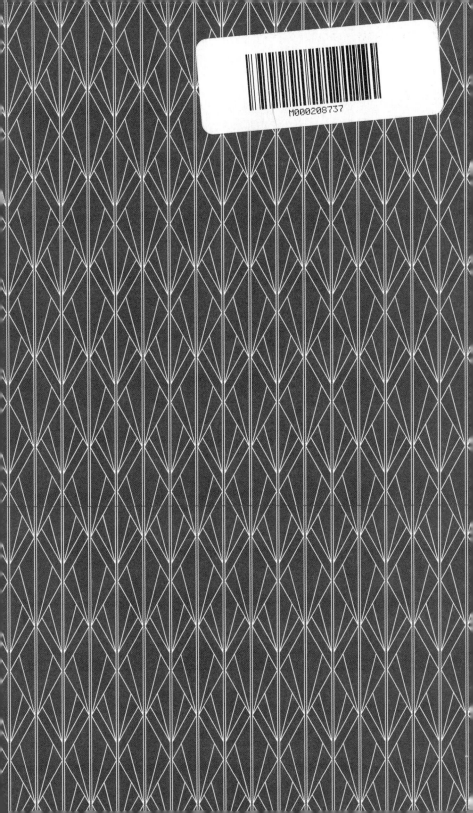

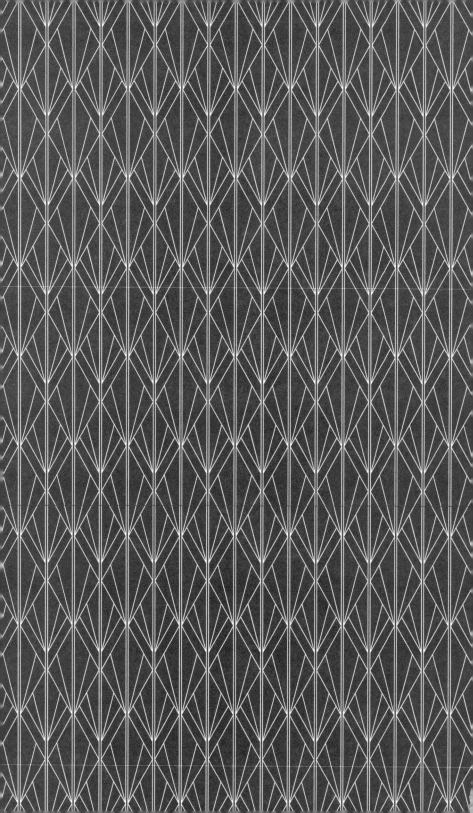

STAYING POWER

A Guided Journal to Living Changed, Connected, and Confident

SARAH JAKES ROBERTS

THOMAS NELSON
Since 1798

Staying Power

© 2024 Sarah Jakes Roberts

Some of the material in this book is from *Power Moves: Ignite Your Confidence & Become a Force*, © 2024 Sarah Jakes Roberts.

Published in Nashville, Tennessee, by Thomas Nelson. Thomas Nelson is a registered trademark of HarperCollins Christian Publishing, Inc.

The author is represented by the Dupree Miller Agency.

Photos of the author are by Cyndi Brown. The remaining images are used under license from Shutterstock.com.

Thomas Nelson titles may be purchased in bulk for educational, business, fund-raising, or sales promotional use. For information, please email SpecialMarkets@ThomasNelson.com.

Unless otherwise noted, Scripture quotations are taken from the New King James Version®. Copyright © 1982 by Thomas Nelson. Used by permission. All rights reserved.

Scripture quotations marked NIV are taken from the Holy Bible, New International Version®, NIV®. Copyright © 1973, 1978, 1984, 2011 by Biblica, Inc.® Used by permission of Zondervan. All rights reserved worldwide. www.zondervan.com. The "NIV" and "New International Version" are trademarks registered in the United States Patent and Trademark Office by Biblica, Inc.®

Any internet addresses, phone numbers, or company or product information printed in this book are offered as a resource and are not intended in any way to be or to imply an endorsement by Thomas Nelson, nor does Thomas Nelson vouch for the existence, content, or services of these sites, phone numbers, companies, or products beyond the life of this book.

ISBN 978-1-4002-3783-8 (HC)

Printed in Canada

24 25 26 27 28 FR 10 9 8 7 6 5 4 3 2 1

CONTENTS

INTRODUCTION

Just as a mighty storm or a streak of lightning leaves an impression, so does power. It's a force we recognize in nature, in our leaders, in our daily lives, and most importantly, in our relationship with God. His power, unlike lightning in a storm, is unwavering, steadfast, and perpetually available to us.

We often wonder how to tap into this power, how to direct it toward realizing our dreams, and that is precisely the intention behind *Staying Power*. As we travel together through this journal, my hope is to help you comprehend and harness your unique force. Because you indeed are a force in the making.

"A force in the making" isn't just a catchy slogan, it's a recognition of your divine potential to effect change, a nod to the dynamic work in progress you are. Like in my book *Power Moves*, which this journal is based on, I explore the idea of becoming a force and how it is directly tied to your inner confidence and ability to solve real-world problems.

Don't be mistaken, becoming a force does not mean being ostentatious or loud. It is about how you make a difference, whether that is stepping up on a global stage or showing empathy in a one-on-one conversation. It is about finding the courage to live a life that resonates with your truest self, becoming an agent of change in your own unique way.

The objective of this journal is straightforward: to guide you toward a life that is changed, connected, and confident. It is about being open to transformations, seeking meaningful connections, and nurturing a deep-seated confidence that allows you to harness this change to benefit your life and those around you.

Through this journal, my hope is to stand by you as you navigate your journey, assisting you in uncovering truths about yourself, in identifying and overcoming obstacles, and in activating your innate power. So join me, at your own pace, as we delve into questions that will guide you toward greater self-awareness and understanding.

I am excited for you to embark on this journey, one that will lead to a life that is enriched with confidence, courage, and a sense of purpose. While you journey, remember to always ask questions and be open to receiving the wisdom God is ready to share with you.

Just remember, you are a force in the making, and I am here rooting for you every step of the way.

CHAPTER 1

CLAMPED DOWN

LET US LAY ASIDE EVERY WEIGHT, AND
THE SIN WHICH SO EASILY ENSNARES
US, AND LET US RUN WITH ENDURANCE
THE RACE THAT IS SET BEFORE US.

HEBREWS 12:1

A few months into living in our home, my husband and I hopped into bed after a long day. We were ready to unwind with an episode of our favorite show. I grabbed the remote and pointed it at the television. Nothing happened. Through a process of elimination, I could confidently say the problem wasn't the remote, and it wasn't the outlet. The problem was actually inside the television.

What was so interesting about the TV no longer working was not that it lacked power. The power was flowing, but there was something internally keeping the TV from converting the power into function.

If you've ever been in an environment where you've felt incapable of demonstrating confidence, you may be more like the busted TV than you realize. Fortunately, there's a secret advantage to being like that television that should give you more of a sense of relief than exasperation. The television had access to power. Since the issue was with the device, our focus could be on converting the power it had access to into power to function in the way it was designed to function.

Your breath is evidence that power is still accessible to you. If you have breath, you have access. Right now, in this very moment, power from God is on and flowing in your direction.

RELEASE THE PRESSURE

No matter how you feel right now, you're not irreparably broken, incapable, or inadequate. The ultimate limitation you're experiencing is the result of constant internal and external pressure to conform, stay silent, perform, or achieve. When that pressure is never released, it eventually ends up having more power to stop you than you have to break free from it.

Right now, in this very moment, power from God is on and flowing in your direction.

Name an area of your life where you're feeling pressure to:

Conform

_____

_____

_____

_____

_____

_____

Stay silent

_____

_____

_____

_____

_____

_____

Perform

_____

_____

_____

_____

_____

Achieve

_____

_____

_____

_____

Releasing the pressure and learning to be powerful does not have to come at the expense of trampling on opportunities and connections you value. You can walk in power, love, humility, and kindness all at the same time. Jesus is a beautiful example of this truth. It's essential that you become discontent with the way things are and hungry for what could be so we can work together to get you to the most powerful you.

You're going to break through what has limited you. . . . You're a force in the making.

Are you discontent with the way things are? Take a moment to jot down the things you long to see change.

_____

_____

_____

_____

_____

You're going to break through what has limited you—armed with the power to never be limited again. You're a force in the making.

COURAGEOUSLY AUTHENTIC

A wide range of culprits zap our power. Here are a few signs that can indicate you're experiencing a loss of power. Check the circles for the ones you can relate to:

- O You find yourself habitually conforming to ideas that sharply contrast with what you really want or believe.
- O You feel frustrated when asked to fulfill obligations that you set the precedent to complete.

- You feel resentful at other people's ability to freely express themselves.
- You find yourself overreacting to trivial issues.
- You feel a constant longing and discontentment.
- You choose appeasing others over advocating for yourself.
- You feel trapped inside your life, regardless of how many things should be sources of joy.
- You feel annoyed when people speak, especially incorrectly, on your behalf or about you in your presence.

Now is not the time to lament over the power you've lost. This is an opportunity to acknowledge and accept that the loss of power is a gift. It makes space for you to seek a connection to our all-powerful God who refills, restores, and refuels you in the place where you experienced loss. The dilemma then is not how to take up space and make demands on ourselves and others so our authentic selves can come back to life. Instead, our journeys revolve around us returning to an uninhibited version of ourselves that is not in a struggle for power because we recognize our authenticity *is* power.

REFLECT ON YOUR FEARS

We can't determine the external variables that have clamped you down until you're willing to acknowledge the fears you think change will bring. Your fears have the power to keep you stuck, but the beginning of disarming that fear is when you dare to confront it with intention.

As much as I'd like you to be able to dive right in to being your most confident, powerful self, I also know lasting change takes time. Taking time to reflect is how we will lay the foundation.

What are you afraid will happen if the power you long for becomes the power you embody?

_____

_____

_____

Reflect on a powerless moment you experienced in your day. What would choosing power have looked like?

_____

_____

_____

Let's begin the journey where you work on realigning your focus, thoughts, and energy to your authenticity and allowing it all to overflow into your purpose, personal community, and ambitions. For now this work is an inside job between you and God.

CHAPTER 2

CAN AGAIN

**FEAR NOT, FOR I AM WITH YOU; BE NOT
DISMAYED, FOR I AM YOUR GOD. I WILL
STRENGTHEN YOU, YES, I WILL HELP YOU, I WILL
UPHOLD YOU WITH MY RIGHTEOUS RIGHT HAND.**

ISAIAH 41:10

Most of the time we're all navigating the reality that we're strong in one space but weak in another. That's why being powerless can be so debilitating. Too often we settle for only functioning in areas where power comes easily and it's easy to refuel.

In what areas of your life does power come easily? For example: friendship, motherhood, self-care, experiencing joy, receiving feedback, and so on.

_____

_____

_____

_____

_____

What are some of the things you do to restore power when you feel it decreasing? For example: practicing positive affirmations, taking a nap, reading a scripture, unplugging, or signing up for an adventure.

_____

_____

_____

_____

When our power tank has a hole in it, though, those methods don't work as well. Far too often they only offer a temporary power surge that depletes us almost as quickly as it charged us.

Where have you noticed you feel determined and focused in the moment, but once you're no longer in the environment, you go back to feeling restricted?

_____

_____

_____

_____

You need power that emits from your spirit and gives momentum to all you do. With this analogy in mind, how would the gauge on your power tank read for all those different ways you show up in your world?

Write a list of all the responsibilities you have to yourself and others. Then beside each one, on a scale of 1 to 5 (with 1 being no pressure and 5 being the max), gauge how empowered you feel to accomplish those obligations. Take note of the areas where you're full. How'd you get there? What is challenging about the places where you feel empty?

_____

_____

_____

_____

God has power in reserve with you in mind. All you have to do is align your heart and mind to receive what's already yours.

POWER IN RESERVE

GOD WON'T GIVE YOU AN ASSIGNMENT HE WILL NOT EMPOWER YOU TO ACCOMPLISH.

Who would you be if you leaned into that statement? What fear would subside, and which doubt would die if you truly trusted that for everything God has assigned you to accomplish, He's also reserved the power for you to get done?

_____

_____

_____

_____

_____

_____

_____

God has power in reserve with you in mind. All you have to do is align your heart and mind to receive what's already yours.

Imagine having a fresh flow of ability, the type of ability that makes completing whatever responsibility that lies ahead of you effortless. Jot down what that might look like.

_____

_____

_____

_____

BREAK UP WITH YOU

Whenever you are not your authentic self with people, you are choosing to allow someone to settle on a false idea of who you are. No matter how subtle their misunderstanding may seem, if you allow them to make it truth, you are accepting a role as an impostor.

How have you been celebrated, esteemed, and acknowledged for who you pretend to be? Do you find yourself mimicking the thoughts and opinions of whoever you desire to please?

_____

_____

_____

_____

_____

When you truly deem yourself worthy, powerful, intelligent, and valuable, you do not easily cave in to the pressure of who other people believe you should be. The only reason your power is not present is because you did not believe, or were not aware, you possessed it in the first place.

Are you letting people and situations rob you of power you have the authority to control? How do you tend to relinquish power on small levels?

_____

_____

_____

_____

_____

God did not make you in His image for you to limit yourself to one expression of who you are. You are broad, bountiful, nuanced, peculiar, simple, elusive, and blatant—just like your Creator. You can be consistently authentic and complex at the same time.

NO MORE CAN'T

We only think we can't do something when we don't have enough personal evidence of a *can't* becoming a *can*.

What is an area in your life where you want something but you have disqualified yourself with a *can't*? Write your want first and then your *can't*.

_____

_____

_____

_____

Another crazy possibility you may have never considered is that God wants the same thing for you as you want for yourself. What would it look like in your life if what you want is actually the thing God has been waiting for you to want?

_____

_____

_____

_____

FEELINGS MATTER

My prayer life became much more intimate when I was able to connect to the truth of what I was feeling by using specific words like *sorrow, agitated, insignificant, hopeful, creative, valued,* and so many more. Underneath most of the things we can't do is a feeling we're trying to avoid.

- O *I want to write the book, but I don't think I can survive feeling embarrassed.*
- O *I want to move, but I am nervous about failing or being alone.*
- O *I want to date, but I don't think I can survive another disappointment.*

Take this opportunity to invite God into a corner of your heart you rarely visit so you can release the frustration, anger, tears, and disappointment that come from not getting what you wanted. Then, because God loves you so much, He'll show you, in that very same space, what He offers you instead. Journal here what God speaks to your heart.

_____

_____

_____

_____

Just because it's not easy doesn't mean it's not possible.

Embracing a *can* mentality is not just about giving your-self permission to do something. A *can* mentality is also giving yourself permission to feel something: "I can feel sad. I can feel joy. I can feel ambitious. I can feel tired. I can feel excited."

Living with the confidence that you can endure hard things makes you resilient. When we no longer have the power to generate resiliency, our decision-making centers around avoiding disappointment or difficult outcomes.

Just because it's not easy doesn't mean it's not possible.

CHAPTER 3

FULLY INTEGRATED

BE STRONG AND OF GOOD COURAGE, FOR TO THIS PEOPLE YOU SHALL DIVIDE AS AN INHERITANCE THE LAND WHICH I SWORE TO THEIR FATHERS TO GIVE THEM. ONLY BE STRONG AND VERY COURAGEOUS, THAT YOU MAY OBSERVE TO DO ACCORDING TO ALL THE LAW WHICH MOSES MY SERVANT COMMANDED YOU; DO NOT TURN FROM IT TO THE RIGHT HAND OR TO THE LEFT, THAT YOU MAY PROSPER WHEREVER YOU GO.

JOSHUA 1:6–7

One of the challenges we face in igniting our confidence and becoming a force is we're constantly being told what to value, how to think, what should upset us, how we should feel about our appearance, how we should work, and so much more.

I want to help you shape your core values so you have a benchmark by which to hold yourself accountable. This process will help you decide what core values should become a staple in your identity—your personal brand. Those values will serve as the standard for your personal integrity. Core values will determine how you make decisions and who you choose to live life with. I believe every person should have at least three to five core values that show up in all they do.

What values do you need to possess so you can have the powerful life you envision?

_____

_____

_____

_____

_____

We are never in a stage of life when we should not be considering what values we want to possess in the many roles we may fulfill. My quest for values begins with my relationship with God. Through prayer, worship, and studying Scripture I can pinpoint what needs to be my priority as I experience the constant transitions of life.

OPEN FOR DEPOSITS

My desire to align my identity with God's intention for my life is a heart posture—a core value I possess regardless of the environment.

You may value self-care, but your programming is not currently set up to allow you to make room for yourself. Instead of breaking out of the system, you become resentful and frustrated. You may value the connection of friends and family, but the pursuit of stability and success makes it difficult for you to honor those values.

You've heard the notion that if a person wanted to do something, they would. It suggests if you're more valuable to them than their demanding schedule or pursuit of their goals, they will make time for you. I believe this argument holds some truth, but I also know firsthand how challenging it is to channel what you value into your actions.

Your systems are wired in your brain, but your core values exist in your heart. Your mind must work to channel the values in your heart into a system that allows them to show up in your life. Part of us feeling frustrated in our identity has to do with our inability to channel what we value in our hearts into our present realities.

A struggle ensues because we're navigating two types of values: staple and situational. Our staple values are the ones that are a constant to us. These may include things like our relationship with God, long-standing friendships with others, and health and wellness. Then we have situational values that center on what a particular stage of our life requires. For example, a student may value mastering certain information while they're in college.

Write down your staple values. Then list your situational values.

_____

_____

_____

_____

_____

_____

_____

_____

The simple prayer of asking God, _What do You need me to see, and who do You need me to be?_ has been my way of harmonizing my staple value of being aligned with God with the reality that things are always changing, and so what I value may need to change too.

Do you have a staple value that says your heart is open to God? Without that, other strong values cannot take root in your life. The first step to forming a solid set of values is releasing your grip on what you thought had value and opening your heart to the values God desires you to have.

Take a moment to ask God, *What do You need me to see, and who do You need me to be?* **Journal what He lays on your heart.**

_____

_____

_____

_____

_____

_____

When you say those words with faith that God has an answer, you become sensitive to how your environment is working with God to answer your needs.

SEARCHING SCRIPTURE

Once your heart has been opened, the search for the answer can begin. I start my search with Scripture. I've learned so much about how God has reshaped, reframed, or rebuked the values of people through His Word. I've never been faced with a situation that didn't have an answer in the Bible.

What need are you experiencing right now?

_____

_____

_____

_____

_____

Take a few minutes to open your Bible or Google a verse that speaks to that theme. Skim through the verses until you find one that pricks your heart. Jot it down here.

_____

_____

_____

_____

_____

If you truly believe that God is all-knowing and all-powerful, when you lean into His vision for your values, you are being positioned to access the most powerful version of yourself for the task at hand. What you value determines how you show up, and how you show up determines what doors are open to you.

CHAPTER 4

THE ECOSYSTEM OF YOU

> HAVE I NOT COMMANDED YOU? BE STRONG
> AND OF GOOD COURAGE; DO NOT BE AFRAID,
> NOR BE DISMAYED, FOR THE LORD YOUR
> GOD IS WITH YOU WHEREVER YOU GO.
>
> *JOSHUA 1:9*

Has anyone ever told you to abandon your comfort zone? There's a reason we stay nice and cozy in our safe places. It's because we know how everything works there. Your comfort zone was constructed by an architect called *survival.* It took note of how engaging or avoiding certain topics made you feel safe or alone. It convinced you that avoiding challenges or opportunities that require vulnerability would give you control and longevity.

When all these ideas began to work together, it created the framework of you. In this realm, rejection, isolation, or unbearable intimacy is decreased significantly because outcomes are predictable. When guesswork is removed from outcomes, we have successfully programmed an existence we are confident won't harm us. But just because it's not harming us doesn't mean it's helping us.

In what ways are you discontent with your comfort zone?

_____

_____

_____

_____

_____

_____

_____

What would it feel like to break free?

_____

_____

_____

_____

_____

_____

You shouldn't take a bold, adventurous leap of faith until you've taken the time to understand your programming. Otherwise, you'll take the leap of faith but leap right back into your comfort zone when the outcomes become too unpredictable.

What situations are guaranteed to make you feel the following?

Ashamed

_____

_____

_____

_____

_____

_____

Fearful

_____

_____

_____

_____

_____

Successful

_____

_____

_____

_____

_____

Prideful

_____

_____

_____

_____

_____

_____

_____

Powerful

_____

_____

_____

_____

_____

_____

_____

ELEMENTS OF YOUR PROGRAMMING

The beliefs, perceptions, and relationships that construct our comfort zones don't just appear out of nowhere. Those materials are accessible because they are readily available in our cultural environments. They were within reach when you needed to make decisions about love, success, responsibility, and integrity.

Consider the elements of your upbringing that shaped your programming. Briefly describe your family of origin. What was your experience of safety and belonging?

_____

_____

_____

_____

Describe the culture you were raised in.

_____

_____

_____

_____

How would you describe the environment of your places
of employment earlier in your life?

_____

_____

_____

_____

_____

When you think of your closest friends growing up, what
feelings come up for you?

_____

_____

_____

_____

_____

_____

You built a world of safety and predictability based on the dangers that were present then, but it's possible you're using programming for a circumstance that no longer exists.

Where might you be programmed to fear scarcity, loneliness, laziness, or lack?

_____

_____

_____

_____

_____

What comforting wiring from the past do you need to break so you can receive an update from God?

_____

_____

_____

SAME OLD SYSTEM

I want to spend some time talking about the systems you're navigating in your environment. But before we get into that, I'd like to explore the internal systems of your heart, mind, and soul. Your internal systems will help you understand the role you play in those external systems.

Think of your internal space like an ecosystem. Within one ecosystem are several systems functioning at once. An ecosystem is simply a community or group of living organisms that live in and interact with each other in a specific environment.

When we recognize how our individuality interconnects with the ecosystem of our families, friends, community, and professional world, we start to understand why staying in our comfort zones is so appealing.

How many systems are at play in the ecosystem of you? Who are the people in those ecosystems?

_____

_____

_____

_____

_____

_____

Out of consideration for the people in your ecosystem who you presume would be adversely affected by you changing, you may be choosing to stay the same. But in considering them, you have alienated yourself.

If you began moving in greater power, who do you feel you would disappoint?

_____

_____

_____

_____

_____

DIVE INTO YOU

Identify a system you desire to change and the role you play in the system. What is one small change you'd like to introduce?

_____

_____

_____

Consider the recurring moments throughout your day when you feel your power is being zapped. Jot them down here.

_____

_____

_____

_____

_____

What new habit have you committed to introducing into your schedule, but the moment you get stressed, you abandon the new habit and fall back into negative behavior?

_____

_____

_____

_____

Maybe it's not that you have weak willpower but rather that you have a system of stress in your life that prohibits you from achieving your desired goal.

If it's too difficult to understand your own system, zoom out of the picture and consider the system of your family. How do they communicate disappointment? How is anger expressed? What are the expectations regarding work ethic and financial responsibility?

_____

_____

_____

If you have made a decision to do things differently and still can't define your system, I'll pose one simple question to you: What would you intentionally do differently to ensure you do not repeat what you experienced in the past?

_____

_____

_____

_____

May God grant you the wisdom to be patient with those who need time to adjust, and may you keep a distance from those who would destroy your growth. There are few things more empowering than being able to identify and qualify the systems that are running your life.

CHAPTER 5

BELIEVE DIFFERENTLY

DO NOT BE CONFORMED TO THIS WORLD, BUT BE TRANSFORMED BY THE RENEWING OF YOUR MIND, THAT YOU MAY PROVE WHAT IS THAT GOOD AND ACCEPTABLE AND PERFECT WILL OF GOD.

ROMANS 12:2

The systems that render you stagnant and ashamed are made powerless only when a stronger, more powerful belief is introduced. A new belief introduces a healthier, more powerful system.

I am only able to receive relief from my negative belief system when I dare to trust that God does not run out of grace when I mess up. When I trust that I am loved beyond measure, it breaks me out of the system that cripples me.

NEW CONVICTIONS

Confront the ugly strongholds of your systems with the knowledge that God's not finished with the masterpiece of you. If you are up against it, it is because God made you to conquer it.

Look behind the protection you keep in place to guard your heart, and start labeling the parts of your systems. Consider a recent outcome, whether it was the outcome you desired or one that fueled your negative paradigm. What were the ingredients of this outcome?

_____

_____

_____

_____

_____

_____

If you are up against it,
it is because God made you
to conquer it.

Don't just focus on the parts that are frustrating. What parts of your system are you proud of? For example, do you have initiative, focus, determination, or discipline?

_____

_____

_____

_____

_____

What would it take for you to get to a positive outcome on a regular basis?

_____

_____

_____

_____

_____

You don't just need a different outcome. You need new convictions. You need a system that is rooted in love, compassion, worthiness, and the pursuit of heaven touching earth through you.

ON THE ALTAR

Heaven touched earth through the life of Esther in the Old Testament. She was a beautiful young woman who had found a way to survive by denying her heritage as a Jew. Even when she was chosen to be the concubine of the Persian king, she maintained her disguise.

It wasn't until the Jews were threatened that she had some tough decisions to make. Once Esther took the time to weigh her options, she chose to break out of the system that had offered her peace and to align with the path that would require her to stand on her truth.

In the end, Esther approached the king and saved her people. She chose power over the illusion of peace and became a force. You're going to have to do the same.

Where have you chosen an illusion of peace that requires you to stifle your authenticity?

_____

_____

_____

_____

_____

You can build the walls to protect yourself, or you can trust that God has placed a forcefield around you.

Imagine how empowered you will be when you're able to maintain the life you love and hang on to your truth at the same time.

Imagine how empowered you will be when you're able to maintain the life you love and hang on to your truth at the same time. Where might God take your either-or mentality and place you in a position to see that it is a both-and? Journal your thoughts here.

_____

_____

_____

_____

_____

A BOTH-AND PARADIGM

You don't have to choose between being a strong friend and a delicate lover. You don't have to pick whether you'll shatter ceilings or make homemade breads. You can be the life of the party *and* a pillar of wisdom. You don't have to relegate power to one expression while diminishing the fullness of your identity.

So often we wonder, *What do I need to do to stop the cycle?* Maybe instead what we need to be asking is, *What do I need to believe?* Or even more powerful, *What belief do I need to release?* I want you to build an altar for the belief system you have uncovered while working through this chapter.

An altar is a sacred structure where gifts or sacrifices are made to God. If you're like me, you want to give God something that feels like a worthy accolade, adorned with the accoutrements of success that are meaningful to our culture. What God wants instead is for us to give up the beliefs that keep us from true relationship with Him.

What limiting beliefs are you holding on to that make you feel disqualified from being treasured by God?

_____

_____

_____

_____

_____

Spend some time in prayer, bringing those limiting beliefs before God. Recognize that He doesn't want you to just lay down the belief system that no longer serves you. He wants to give you something in exchange. What do you sense that is?

_____

_____

_____

CONNECT AND CULTIVATE

Scripture reveals to us that God is a healer, a provider, a comforter, a lover, a companion, and so much more. When you experience that, it's God's way of winking at you. Those who encountered Jesus were left enamored because, in a world full of hate, distraction, rules, and restrictions, there was someone who took the time to care, heal, refresh, and restore them from the inside out.

If you can experience the connection and conviction of God, you can be trusted with power.

As you begin this journey of eliminating the toxic system that has become familiar, your relationship with God will be your compass. Let Him push you into the next dimension of your power.

Choose one of these "more powerful than" statements and place it somewhere you will see every day.

- O I believe vulnerability is more powerful than silence.
- O I believe hope is more powerful than shame.
- O I believe joy is more powerful than pain.
- O I believe the present is more powerful than the past.
- O I believe dignity is more powerful than acceptance.
- O I believe attempting is more powerful than regretting.
- O I believe discipline is more powerful than doubt.

O I believe humility is more powerful than
  perfectionism.
O I believe faith is more powerful than fear.
O I believe wholeness is more powerful than
  loneliness.

CHAPTER 6

THE MEASURING STICK

> WE DARE NOT CLASS OURSELVES OR COMPARE OURSELVES WITH THOSE WHO COMMEND THEMSELVES. BUT THEY, MEASURING THEMSELVES BY THEMSELVES, AND COMPARING THEMSELVES AMONG THEMSELVES, ARE NOT WISE. WE, HOWEVER, WILL NOT BOAST BEYOND MEASURE, BUT WITHIN THE LIMITS OF THE SPHERE WHICH GOD APPOINTED US.
>
> *2 CORINTHIANS 10:12–13*

Your core values are the measuring stick that determines whether you're living up to who you can be. Your ability to live within those principles determines whether you're living a life of integrity. When you compare the daily choices you make to the measuring stick of your values, you can see how you're growing your personal brand.

Too often we are content not living up to our values. We give ourselves so much grace that we are impotent at developing the character and spirituality that allow us to be powerful on this earth. I'm not suggesting you no longer have compassion for yourself when you miss the mark, but I want your compassion to lead to determination.

God is compassionate about what makes us stumble and is compassionate about us getting back up again. Yes, you should have grace for yourself, but you should be leery of lingering too long in defeat.

In what area of your life does it feel as if you've lingered too long?

_____

_____

_____

_____

_____

_____

What would it feel like to let grace overwhelm you even when you have stumbled?

_____

_____

_____

_____

_____

_____

TODAY IMPACTS TOMORROW

If tomorrow is not promised, how do you want to show up today? What values do you want to be fully aligned with your words and actions?

Commitment to relentlessly living a life aligned with your principles is how you develop integrity. I want you to begin the journey of truly establishing your values.

It's important you make this a part of your daily practice. When marinating on the choices you've made throughout the day and whether they aligned with your values, try to reserve judgment and excuse making.

Commitment to relentlessly living a life aligned with your principles is how you develop integrity.

In what ways did you need to show up today? What different set of values did you have to rotate based on the environment and the individuals in front of you?

_____

_____

_____

_____

With a simple yes or no, determine if you had a value-aligned day. If the answer is yes, commend yourself. Acknowledge the fact that you were able to honor God's Word on who you were supposed to be in that moment.

If the answer is no, ask yourself these questions: What made it difficult to live up to your values? Did you get angry? Were you tired? Did you feel shamed? Were you stressed?

_____

_____

_____

_____

_____

A mindset that takes advantage of grace may say, *Oh, well. I'm human. This will probably happen again. I do well in all these other areas, so I should be able to slide in this area.* The problem with relying solely on grace is that it disguises pride. When your ego convinces you that living outside of your values is permissible, you miss out on an opportunity for humility to welcome love and compassion from the person most affected by your actions.

Compassion offers a much more honest reckoning. It says, "You have been functioning without being refueled by rest and vision for so long you can't even see yourself. You should apologize first to yourself for living outside of your values and then to those who've been affected by your inner disconnect."

Integrity is not just about honoring the people in your life. It's about honoring yourself too.

How do you think you'll feel with more integrity in your life? What are the good outcomes you may experience?

_____

_____

_____

_____

_____

_____

Integrity is not just about honoring the people in your life. It's about honoring yourself too.

FULLY INTEGRATED

Cultivating a relationship with God and leaning into the values that draw you closer to Him will allow the most powerful you to emerge. When you set out to live according to those values, your life is not centered around living up to other people's expectations. Instead it's oriented toward being accountable to who God needs you to be at any given moment.

Sometimes that means the way people have once engaged with you may have to expand to make room for your new journey. That's okay! God does not call you to have values that will alienate you from people He has ordained to be in your life. The more you choose to be accountable to this new journey, the more you will realize how capable you are of making choices that may disappoint other people but elevate you.

In what unhealthy bonds or relationships may you experience some discomfort as you change the way you engage?

_____

_____

_____

_____

_____

The people in your life may have more elasticity than you give them credit for. Give them the chance to meet you where you are instead of overextending yourself to be who they think you are.

Spend some time talking with God about the way of being He wants to establish in you. Journal what He lays on your heart.

_____

_____

_____

_____

_____

I want you to experience the full integration of what it means to be human—tired, tempted, excited, upset, focused, ambitious, and irritated. Jesus experienced all those things but still clung to His values of wanting to please His Father in heaven by establishing His kingdom, restoring the relationship between Creator and creation, and serving as the gateway that allowed heaven to come to earth.

It's important for you to experience the power of living not to be valued by others but rather to become what God sees. That's what made Jesus powerful. That's what will make you powerful.

CHAPTER 7

PROBLEM SOLVER

LET THIS MIND BE IN YOU WHICH WAS ALSO IN CHRIST JESUS, WHO, BEING IN THE FORM OF GOD, DID NOT CONSIDER IT ROBBERY TO BE EQUAL WITH GOD, BUT MADE HIMSELF OF NO REPUTATION, TAKING THE FORM OF A BONDSERVANT, AND COMING IN THE LIKENESS OF MEN. AND BEING FOUND IN APPEARANCE AS A MAN, HE HUMBLED HIMSELF AND BECAME OBEDIENT TO THE POINT OF DEATH, EVEN THE DEATH OF THE CROSS.

PHILIPPIANS 2:5–8

You can do all the internal work in the world, but until you are ready to allow your inner work to be on display, you'll never see how much of a masterpiece you have become.

Confidence is an inside job, but you become a force when your confidence gives you the courage to be a solution to what's happening around you. If your confidence is restricted to just making you feel good about yourself, you've stopped short of what it means to truly have confidence. Jesus said, "I have come down from heaven not to do my will but to do the will of him who sent me" (John 6:38 NIV). Jesus' confidence was not just rooted in what He could do. It was rooted in the knowledge of who He was because of who sent Him in the first place.

Where do you tend to put your confidence? Here are some common areas: control over circumstances, personal appearance, money and status, achievement, others' approval, and pleasure.

_____

_____

_____

_____

_____

I want you to have the type of confidence that pushes you in the direction of what you once thought was impossible. Confidence is not about having the right circumstances. Confidence is trusting that you work wherever God sends you, regardless of the circumstances.

Confidence is trusting
that you work wherever
God sends you,
regardless of the
circumstances.

When you know who you are, you don't allow bad seeds to hijack your identity. You recognize that what you do is the organic byproduct of who you are.

God did not call you to success without scars. What would it look like for you to trust that God has called you to the sacred journey of trusting Him through failure and disappointment?

_____

_____

_____

_____

_____

HIDDEN DEVELOPMENT

The old voices of fear and shame that once haunted and taunted you will surrender to the knowledge that you have been made whole. You will be informing your doubt, worry, shame, and fear that power has moved, and you're determined to move with it.

Hidden development lays the foundation for you to become a force. When you reconcile your life, you begin to trust God's ability to see you through any trial, and you have confidence in your patience while God goes ahead of you.

What is one thing you could do this week to not just be a viewer but a force, actively engaging in a way that the earth looks different because of your presence?

_____

_____

_____

_____

_____

_____

It's hard to get to this stage of confidence when we're consumed with our need for deliverance from our fears and insecurities, but once you get a taste of partnering with God to make the world better, you can never forget that level of fulfillment. What's happening inside you must come out so the world can experience light where there was once darkness.

ANSWER THE PROBLEM

There is no doubt we are not short on problems these days. Turning on the news or opening an app will reveal in a heartbeat the depravity of the world. We can allow this to discourage us, or we can see it as a clarion call to

I am not just a citizen.
I am a solution.

engage. Remember that question I ask God when walking into a new space? *What do You need me to see, and who do You need me to be?*

I don't just limit this to the rooms I walk into. I ask this when I see headlines that trouble my soul. I am not just a citizen. I am a solution.

Do you sense that your gifts and talents could bring order and restoration where things are in disarray? If so, where do you think God could use you to do that?

_____

_____

_____

_____

_____

_____

I believe God wants your life to be happy and your soul to thrive, but part of being in any good relationship is asking the other person, "What I can do for you?" When we think this way, we may realize that God wants to use the injuries of our past to help someone nurse their own wounds.

It's so important that you make your growth about you for a season so that later it can be about the world you're called to serve for a lifetime. People who tell you it's not about you stunt your ability to truly multiply your gifts. You need to have a season where you turn your focus inward. When you dissect what tried to kill you, you're able to better guide others through, or away from, the pitfalls that had you bound.

What problem are you constantly seeing? Maybe it's an issue in your family, organization, community, school, or church.

_____

_____

_____

_____

_____

_____

_____

_____

Are you waiting on someone to fix something you're bothered by, or are you willing to risk error to be the solution? Ask God what role you can play in the solution. Journal your thoughts here.

_____

_____

_____

_____

_____

_____

_____

_____

God doesn't make mistakes, but in the pursuit of discovering why He created you, you will certainly make mistakes. That's okay. The Holy Spirit is waiting to fill your heart with His wisdom and lessons even in loss. I truly believe for every soul there is a solution waiting to happen.

CHAPTER 8

FILL THE EARTH

> **GOD BLESSED [ADAM AND EVE], AND GOD SAID TO THEM, "BE FRUITFUL AND MULTIPLY; FILL THE EARTH AND SUBDUE IT; HAVE DOMINION OVER THE FISH OF THE SEA, OVER THE BIRDS OF THE AIR, AND OVER EVERY LIVING THING THAT MOVES ON THE EARTH."**
>
> *GENESIS 1:28*

God's original intention was for earth to take on the attributes of heaven. He gave Adam and Eve a formula for how to make that happen, but sin's entrance built a wall that made earth become a slow-cooker mixture of heaven, hell, humanity, fear, decadence, and pain. Now, if I were God, I would've gone about my business like earth was an ex who missed out on the best thing that could have happened to them. No surprise that God is better than me.

He did not give us what we deserved.

He did not give up on who we could become.

God did not let go of the notion that heaven could still find a home on earth. He just realized we were going to need some support to get it done. Jesus came to restore the bridge between heaven and earth.

In what areas of your life would you like to see fruit multiplying?

_____

_____

_____

_____

_____

_____

_____

How can you make sure the fruit of your life doesn't end with you? What would it look like for you to be a seed thrower?

_____

_____

_____

_____

_____

_____

_____

Anytime you give your wisdom, serve another person, share a comforting post, or offer a listening ear, you are multiplying God's image on earth.

YOUR FUNDAMENTAL BASE

By being exiled from the garden, the place where Adam and Eve started would not be the place they landed. I love when a scripture gives us insight into the character

Even when God holds you accountable, He doesn't forsake you or abandon you.

of God: He knows we need a solid base before we can reasonably expand.

The work you've done regarding your systems and values is not just about novel ideas. You have been establishing a firm foundation so you can build without fear of demolition. When Adam and Eve were banished from the garden, they lost life as they'd known it. But they didn't lose the fundamental base knowledge that even when God holds you accountable, He doesn't forsake you or abandon you.

When have you experienced God's faithfulness at a time when people may have let you down?

_____

_____

_____

_____

_____

_____

MORE THAN MEETS THE EYE

I am convinced that when God looks at our world He's not distracted by the standing structures. He sees the busy souls that are still empty. He sees the bustling cities that are still empty. He sees the full churches with leaders who are still empty.

So how do we fill the earth? We add the substance of our God-inspired growth and development into the conversation.

How can you begin to break through the noisy emptiness of our culture on an individual level?

_____

_____

_____

_____

_____

Where are the gaps in your community and industry? How can you use who you've become to not just promote yourself but fill gaps?

_____

_____

_____

_____

What gift could you be offering the world that we don't even realize we need?

_____

_____

_____

_____

_____

Let me say this before you start minimizing your gift because you think someone else has already brought it to the table: It doesn't matter how many people are doing the thing you do. If God has laid it on your heart to do, it's so you can fill an empty spot.

Where have you let the fear of bringing to the table something that someone else has already brought hold you back from doing what God has laid on your heart?

_____

_____

_____

It doesn't matter how many people are doing the thing you do. If God has laid it on your heart to do, it's so you can fill an empty spot.

Filling the empty places will look different for everyone. There are likely empty places right in your family, friendships, workplaces, and communities.

Write down the ways you have become full and how you could pour into someone else. It could be as simple as sending a card, making a meal, or creating places for connection in environments that can be large and overwhelming.

_____

_____

_____

_____

_____

TAKE YOUR REIGN

I believe God realized that Adam and Eve would experience encounters with species that were stronger and more complex than they might have anticipated. God wanted them to know before they ever saw a lion, tiger, or bear that they had dominion over every living thing that moved on the earth. In other words, God didn't want them to be afraid of beasts.

Few of us are facing off with wildlife the way Adam and Eve had to, but that doesn't mean we don't have our fair share of beasts in everyday life. As you become a force, I will not downplay the reality of beasts that await you. From the outside looking in, they look bigger, stronger, and more resourced than you.

What "beasts" are you encountering right now? What beasts do you anticipate facing in the future?

_____

_____

_____

_____

_____

_____

In 1 John 4:4, John warned believers of the beasts that awaited them. Then he said something that can serve as a shield for you: "You are of God, little children, and have overcome them, because He who is in you is greater than he who is in the world."

When you trust that the greatness of God in you is greater than any beast outside of you, you will have

When you trust that the
greatness of God in you
is greater than any beast
outside of you, you will have
dominion without fear.

dominion without fear. Any beast that stands in the way of what God wants to do in the earth is not just your enemy. It's God's enemy too.

It is not your opposition's responsibility to make room for you. It's your responsibility to become a force that accepts no other option. How does that knowledge change how you view your beasts?

_____

_____

_____

_____

_____

It's time for the power in you to emerge and change what's happening around you.

CHAPTER 9

OUTSIDE FORCES

MY FLESH AND MY HEART FAIL; BUT GOD IS THE STRENGTH OF MY HEART AND MY PORTION FOREVER.

PSALM 73:26

Being powerful is giving yourself permission to be honest about your capabilities, desires, needs, and feelings at any given moment and without judgment. It is permission to live authentically so you can show up without preconceived limitations from yourself or others.

Sometimes being powerful is actually saying you're

True power is not about competing with anyone else. It's daring to truly master yourself.

tired, overwhelmed, angry, confused, or stuck. In a world that applauds relentless productivity, sometimes the most powerful thing you can do is rest. If you only feel powerful when you think you're performing better than someone else, power will always feel like it's slipping through your hands. True power is not about competing with anyone else. It's daring to truly master yourself.

MORE THAN ONE EXPRESSION

When I'm completely tapped into the zone required for me to overcome my nerves and fears to deliver a message, I feel invincible. The moment I finish, I feel like the clock has struck midnight, and my carriage has turned into a pumpkin. I decided that what I was wrestling with was not something my therapist could help me with. This was a conversation between God and me. It didn't take long before I realized that part of the reason I felt a disconnect between the moments I was speaking and the moments I was just going about my everyday life was that I thought power could only have one expression.

What if you released your limited perspective on what power is and how it is expressed? How would it allow you to experience the steady flow of power that is ever present?

_____

_____

_____

_____

_____

How do you feel when you are fully present and engaged in what is happening before you?

_____

_____

_____

_____

When we practice being wholly aware, we can accurately assess how to respond to and connect with whoever or whatever is in front of us. Think of a moment you spent time with someone and reflected afterward that you didn't feel any more connected to them than you did before.

_____

_____

_____

_____

Willing yourself to be present in the moment requires that you shift mentally and emotionally as quickly as your roles do. When you do this, you'll end up bringing the same power of productivity that makes you great at work into the environment of your home or relationships.

Take a moment to jot down all the hats you wear: daughter, sibling, friend, partner, coworker, leader, parent, and so on.

_____

_____

_____

_____

You cannot expect to be powerful at fulfilling a role that is not authentic and natural to who you are. It will exhaust you and render you ineffective at producing change.

What roles don't feel natural right now?

_____

_____

_____

_____

You cannot expect to be powerful at fulfilling a role that is not authentic and natural to who you are.

OVEREXERTION

When I was learning how to do strength training, it dawned on me that the work I was putting in at the gym could not translate into power unless I took the time to stretch, rest, and recover. It's often the thing that doesn't seem like it matters at all that produces our power. For strength training, we produce power through resting and stretching.

Becoming powerful is trusting that the moments when you don't feel like you're doing anything powerful at all may be the moments you are growing the most.

God did not stop being all-powerful on the seventh day when He decided to rest. He just understood what would make Him most powerful for that day was not creating but rather resting.

Do you notice a tendency to overexert yourself? What does that look like?

_____

_____

_____

_____

_____

_____

How would it feel to press into rest more? What emotions come up when you think about that?

_____

_____

_____

_____

_____

_____

To reclaim rest, we must navigate negative systems and destructive industries that have been created to promote and protect specific people. And as if the outside forces weren't enough, we then have to deal with the reality that negative forces are at play within us. The force of our anger, insecurity, anxiety, and ambition must be navigated. The only way we can effectively combat the internal and external forces is to resist the inclination to go mind over matter and push through.

In what area of your life right now do you feel like there is no wind in your sails and you are all out of ability?

_____

_____

_____

_____

_____

What would it look like to rest your decision-making muscles and stretch your faith, rather than lifting heavier and for longer periods of time?

_____

_____

_____

_____

_____

_____

SAME STARTING POINT

Learning to tell when you should be pushing harder and when you should fall back is not easy, but I believe they both have the same starting point. In our relationship with God, we can admit we are in over our heads. In the safety of His counsel, we can say we are overwhelmed by our sea of responsibilities.

**What thoughts go through your head when the pressure
and stress of your life are at an all-time high?**

_____

_____

_____

_____

_____

_____

_____

_____

_____

_____

When sizing up all you're up against, sometimes the best
decision you can make is no decision at all. Take all the
energy you're exerting in making a decision and channel
it into forcing yourself into a space of rest.

What are your fears, adversaries, and insecurities? How can you reclaim your posture of rest in these areas?

_____

_____

_____

_____

_____

_____

_____

_____

_____

My husband introduced me to a friend of his, Phil Munsey, early on in our marriage, and he's always saying, "Your destiny is not going anywhere without you." If nothing is going to pass you by, you can take the time you need to make a decision with clarity.

CHAPTER 10

THE FORCE IS REAL

> SET YOUR MIND ON THINGS ABOVE, NOT ON THINGS ON THE EARTH. FOR YOU DIED, AND YOUR LIFE IS HIDDEN WITH CHRIST IN GOD. WHEN CHRIST WHO IS OUR LIFE APPEARS, THEN YOU ALSO WILL APPEAR WITH HIM IN GLORY.
>
> *COLOSSIANS 3:2–4*

The moment you begin to walk in truth and wisdom, it feels like all kinds of distractions are in your way. You're not going crazy; the force is real. In the moments you begin to feel the resistance and strain from this real opposition, you have an opportunity to enact another force, one that is rooted in a heightened spiritual awareness.

Prayer and worship are the gateways to that awareness and are the most powerful tools we have against the dark forces hoping to stunt our growth. Prayer and worship are how we exercise our authority over evil before we even begin to determine what practical steps we may need to take.

Most of us struggle because we don't always know when we should be leaning into the presence of God or creating a practical strategy for our resources. I believe this happens because we are used to figuring things out by ourselves. There comes a point when the tools we once used are no longer able to produce the most optimal outcome.

Instead of becoming frustrated by our lack of ability to achieve our desired results, we have to go back to the drawing board to make sure God is blessing the method we've chosen to overcome resistance. I know you're wondering, *How do I do this?* The answer is one you're not going to want to hear. Here it is anyway: do nothing.

In what ways are you actively overexerting your knowledge, experience, strength, and passion to procure a particular outcome? Where have you strained yourself trying to build yourself or others?

_____

_____

_____

_____

_____

_____

_____

Resisting the temptation to be the captain of your own ship, or the captain of someone else's, will require focus, dedication, and trust in God above all. From the place of rest, you may recognize where you got off center.

What are some of the distractions in your life that might be agents of your opposition meant to detract from your power and render you unable to focus on your mission?

_____

_____

_____

_____

_____

_____

Resisting the temptation to be the captain of your own ship, or the captain of someone else's, will require focus, dedication, and trust in God above all.

When you set out to accomplish tasks throughout the day, take note of the moments you are distracted from the finish line. Focus on what forces are within your ability to control. Don't judge yourself; this is just an opportunity for inventory. Write them down here. It's possible the same thing may distract you more than once in a day. That's okay. This is a safe space.

_____

_____

_____

_____

_____

_____

_____

_____

OVERPOWER YOUR ENEMY

When temptation gets real, don't pretend it has no power. Instead introduce what has more power.

When temptation gets real, don't pretend it has no power. Instead introduce what has more power.

What are some of the very real temptations you're facing right now? For example, connecting with a person you know isn't healthy, making a purchase your budget doesn't support, gossiping, or responding in anger to someone who has offended you.

_____

_____

_____

_____

_____

_____

_____

Don't just battle temptation in your head. Use your words to push temptation back. Even declaring with a whisper when you can't say it with a yell is enough to serve notice to hell.

Your mind may start to betray you and make you believe you do not have the ability to move in power on earth. You may have a history of defeat that has become a weapon against your destiny, but God can use the words that come out of your mouth to push your enemy back.

Now construct declarations to speak to the temptations you just listed. Here are a couple of examples to get you started: "I no longer want to be someone who finds pleasure in tearing someone down." "I will not allow you to lure me into betraying my peace by acting out of anger."

_____

_____

_____

_____

_____

_____

When you can't put your enemy in its place, the least you can do is refuse to allow your enemy to pull you out of your position. The enemy lures you from focusing on your transformation by tempting you with opportunities that will detract you from development. Those opportunities could be small and seemingly inconsequential, but small compromises become big when you begin to yield.

Eliminate access to one of the things that stunts your development for a set amount of time. It could be as simple as taking a few days away from a toxic book or favorite food. The goal is to break your rhythm long enough for you to see how much more productive and focused you can become.

Instead of focusing on the absence of that thing in your world, fill that space with a moment of prayer and connection with God.

Journal your experience. What did you do, and how did it feel?

_____

_____

_____

_____

_____

_____

_____

_____

The old, powerless version of you has died. You're in the awkward stage of figuring out who you are without pretending to be who you aren't. In those moments remember that when you model a life that looks like Jesus', you'll discover the most powerful version of you.

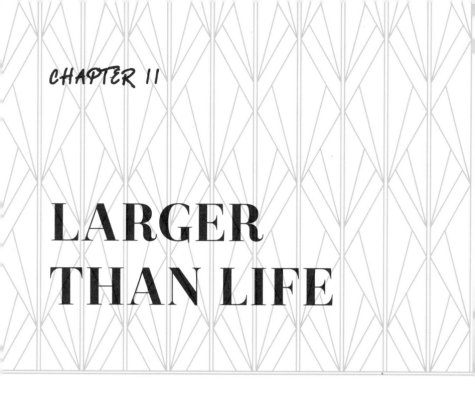

CHAPTER 11

LARGER THAN LIFE

LET NOTHING BE DONE THROUGH SELFISH
AMBITION OR CONCEIT, BUT IN LOWLINESS
OF MIND LET EACH ESTEEM OTHERS BETTER
THAN HIMSELF. LET EACH OF YOU LOOK OUT
NOT ONLY FOR HIS OWN INTERESTS, BUT
ALSO FOR THE INTERESTS OF OTHERS.

PHILIPPIANS 2:3–4

Your power is not just reserved for intense decision-making or organizing chaos. When you embrace that, it means you leave space for rest. When you accept that rest and recovery are also a part of being powerful, you will have to give space for the people in your life to stand tall while you're falling back. It won't always be your time to shine, and when you can move beyond just accepting that to being grateful for it, you'll notice it changes everything.

I'd like you to consider how you can trust that when your power is dormant, someone else's can be active in a way that preserves you and prepares them. What if our insistence on being the one who shows up in power all the time is diminishing us and limiting growth in the people we love?

Some people believe they are the only ones capable of meeting goals and objectives for those in their sphere of influence. These people are frustrated from doing things on their own *and* frustrated when other people do things because those people did not do it the way they would have done it.

Think of someone you know who has relentless determination and commitment to growth. What ups and downs might they be navigating?

_____

_____

_____

_____

_____

Are you in a season right now where it's your time to shine? If not, how would it feel to be grateful for that?

_____

_____

_____

_____

_____

_____

_____

_____

_____

I'm willing to bet that whoever invented the light switch did so because they realized they needed to find a way to choose between power being dormant or active. Otherwise, if the power were left on continuously, it would end up burning out the light bulb on the receiving end.

How could your insistence on being the one who shows up in power all the time be diminishing you and limiting growth in the people you love?

Make a list of some people in your immediate circle. On a scale of 1 to 5 (with 1 being the least and 5 being the most), rate yourself on how much you insist on doing things on your own or in your own way as opposed to their way. Are you helping them or stunting them?

_____

_____

_____

_____

_____

_____

_____

ARRESTING PRIDE

It's subtle, but often pride shows up in our insistence on doing things our way. Pride shows up in how we look down on others for the choices and decisions they've made. It's stealthy when it seeps in, and it's difficult to arrest, but pride blinds us and can prevent us from being compassionate with ourselves and others.

We need to make a real distinction between confidence and pride. Pride is rooted in how much bigger or better you are in comparison to others and, surprisingly, how much bigger and better you can be compared to who you once were. Confidence is rooted in the ability to celebrate the attempts and efforts of others without feeling threatened or being abrasively critical.

Do you sometimes compare yourself to who you once were? How does that make you feel?

_____

_____

_____

_____

_____

_____

I hate to break it to you, but being better than you were yesterday may not be possible. The way life is set up, your yesterday could have been filled with peak adulting behavior—with timeliness, patience, focus, and discipline. Tomorrow you could regress to who you were five years ago with one phone call. On those days, if you lay your head down in shame, then you know that what you're pursuing is not actually confidence but rather pride.

Confidence is not about being flawless.

Spend some time talking to God about the areas where you've regressed. What is He speaking to you about trusting His work in your life and loving every step of your journey while still moving toward progress?

_____

_____

_____

_____

_____

_____

_____

_____

_____

If you can only hold yourself in high regard when you are blind to your flaws, pride has become the architect of your life. Confidence is not about being flawless.

Look for an opportunity this week to intentionally put yourself in a situation where you disengage from things you know you're great at and support someone else's attempt at mastery. You could even take it a step further and ask how you can support them. Give them the space to discover what works best for them. Journal about the experience here.

_____

_____

_____

_____

_____

THE POWER OF THE COLLECTIVE

Nothing happens in our lives that is not affected by someone else's choice or decision. Whether we like to admit it or not, we are experiencing our culture, our projects, and our responsibilities as a collective.

This means there is a possibility that there is someone whose plate is just as full as mine and yet they're finding a way forward too. It also means that nine times out of ten my plate is also lighter because of a load someone else is carrying.

Make a list of some of the people directly connected to the orchestration of your reality. Think all the way from your spouse to government leaders to tech innovators to your children's teachers to the delivery person who brings you packages so you don't have to run to the store. How do these people lighten your load?

_____

_____

_____

_____

_____

It is impossible to do anything on earth without partnership. Navigating the complexities of life will require strategic alliances and partnerships. When those partnerships share the same goal, nothing can stand in their way. Imagine how far you could go if you were cautiously seeking the right partners to help catapult your vision.

Start defining the type of person your vision requires now so you don't miss them when they come. If it's a romantic partner, what are their values? If it's a business partner, what skill set will they bring to the table that expands your vision?

The most powerful thing you'll ever have is a larger-than-life vision that requires you to call in the partners required to make it happen.

CHAPTER 12

JOINING FORCES

> TWO ARE BETTER THAN ONE, BECAUSE THEY HAVE A GOOD REWARD FOR THEIR LABOR. FOR IF THEY FALL, ONE WILL LIFT UP HIS COMPANION. BUT WOE TO HIM WHO IS ALONE WHEN HE FALLS, FOR HE HAS NO ONE TO HELP HIM UP.
>
> *ECCLESIASTES 4:9–10*

We've talked about creating your own core values, but now we get to use those core values to help you better engage with and support the people in your world. I think part of the reason we struggle with truly maximizing the beauty of partnership and relationships is that we spend too much time filling voids.

If we make decisions based on filling a void of friendship, companionship, or productivity, we will be frustrated when the person does not share our values and begins to overdeliver in areas that don't matter while underdelivering what we care about the most.

If you're going to join forces with someone, you have to trust that you and the person have the same shared values.

Journal about a time you tried to partner with someone who did not share your values.

_____

_____

_____

_____

_____

Taking the time to understand a person's values and how they align with your own can ensure that when you join forces you become stronger. By partnering with people who have similar values, I've been able to increase and expand the vision God's given me for my life, family, gifts, talents, and influence in a way that would not have been possible without joining forces.

What area of your life could be amplified by you joining forces? Could your peace be amplified by joining forces with someone else who shares your values?

_____

_____

_____

_____

_____

Pay attention to the moments when God places someone in your world who is walking a similar path as you. What such moments have you noticed this week?

_____

_____

_____

_____

_____

_____

CONFLUENCE OVER INFLUENCE

Too often we run the risk of flowing as individual rivers. We're so content with staying in our own flow that we miss out on the unique gift that occurs when two forces come together. Connecting with another person who is moving with the same sense of purpose, destiny, peace, and power as you is how we experience confluences, a coming together of two streams. Even deeper, merging our lives with God's will is a more transformational river than any confluence on earth.

What would happen if you actively engaged with the people in your world by deciding whether that engagement will form a confluence or zap you of power?

_____

_____

_____

_____

_____

Qualifying our inner circle with a measuring stick of confluence is not about taking advantage of people. It's about understanding and valuing what you bring to the table. It's not as challenging to evaluate the ways a person can make you better as it is to determine the ways you can add value to them. That's why it's critical to have a healthy knowledge of your flaws and strengths.

Take a few minutes to jot down what value you bring to your inner circle.

_____

_____

_____

_____

_____

Consider what brings you health, safety, and security in your relationships and journal about it here.

_____

_____

_____

_____

_____

_____

How can you be strategic about whom you give access to, and how you can avoid constantly re-forming toxic or draining connections?

_____

_____

_____

_____

_____

_____

What criteria do you have for behaviors, conversations, and ethics you desire from the people you allow in your circle? How can these reduce the margin of confusion, disagreement, betrayal, and error?

_____

_____

_____

_____

_____

THE ULTIMATE CONFLUENCE

The beauty of the New Testament is in the lengths that God was willing to go for His creation to experience the ultimate confluence with Him. If we can truly wrap our minds around merging with God, we will understand the foundational framework for every relationship we're in.

How does it make you feel to know the all-powerful, all-knowing, and ever-present God desires to dwell with you? How would it change your outlook on life to know He is there regardless of your weaknesses, ignorance, or disengagement?

God would rather have a trickle from you than nothing at all. He longs to unleash a divine stream of love and wisdom that radically changes your identity.

If we can truly wrap our minds around merging with God, we will understand the foundational framework for every relationship we're in.

Spend some time asking God how He sees you and feels about you. What do you hear Him saying?

_____

_____

_____

_____

_____

Your job is not to get God to change His mind about you. Your job is to search God's mind for His truth about you.

When you begin to confront any separation between you and God, you directly attack the space that doubt, fear, and dark forces exploit.

How do you feel about the goodness of God? In spite of the hard things in your life, do you believe He is good all the time? Or do you find it difficult to fully trust His plan for your life because you struggle to believe He's good?

_____

_____

_____

_____

Your job is not to get God to change His mind about you. Your job is to search God's mind for His truth about you.

If it is your testimony that you're unsure of God's goodness, I'd like to leave you with a thought to consider. Saying that God is good is not the same thing as saying life is good. Saying "God is good" is acknowledging that good has a source, and the source is God. The substance of what God is made up of is so good that even when good faces off against evil, the situation still turns out good. Your invitation to God to meet you, no matter where you are, is inviting good to take over your life.

When good takes over, it empowers you even when life isn't going as planned. You can recognize that your life is not your own but rather a confluence of God's goodness and your weakness working together so heaven can touch earth.

CHAPTER 13

OPEN YOUR MIND

IT IS THE GLORY OF GOD TO CONCEAL A MATTER, BUT THE GLORY OF KINGS IS TO SEARCH OUT A MATTER.

PROVERBS 25:2

We've talked about power moving between our internal thoughts and emotions. We've even discussed the power struggle between humanity and darkness. But as you begin to truly embrace your identity as a force on earth, I want to prepare you for what it feels like to be on the edge of innovation.

Few people truly discuss the loneliness, vulnerability, and second-guessing that comes with being the first one to see that power is shifting from one idea to another.

When you draw closer to God, it doesn't just initiate a journey of bearing God's image on earth; it also grants you access to God's plans for the earth. When you begin to grow in God, He can share more about the complexities and nuances of His plan.

When I set aside the time to truly seek the Holy Spirit in dark seasons, I often find wisdom about why God didn't intervene when I was at my lowest. Sometimes what you're calling darkness, God is calling development.

Recall a dark season in your life. How might what appeared to be darkness have been God developing you?

_____

_____

_____

_____

_____

When you refuse to believe you serve a God who would leave you in the dark, you search scriptures, sermons, worship songs, and meditations until you begin to see light flickering again. The pursuit of God's perspective is not just about reconciling your past and making peace

Sometimes what you're calling darkness, God is calling development.

with your present. God's perspective also carries with it innovation for how your gifts and talents align with what God wants to see happen in the earth.

Going back to the dark season you just wrote about, what "light" has God revealed to you from that time? What has His perspective shown you about who you are and what gifts He's given you?

_____

_____

_____

_____

_____

YOU'RE ON TO SOMETHING

What would it look like to embrace the truth that your existence is innovation? How could your ideas that feel weird, quirky, and maybe a little strange actually be evidence that you're allowing your mind the freedom to live outside of constructs that exist to create conformity?

I am not suggesting that every single idea you possess is something the world needs, because we all know that sometimes we have more ideas than we even have the energy, resources, or time to execute. I am proposing, though, that you should become more comfortable with letting your mind run wild without fear of rejection or the awareness of its oddity.

What is something you use or do every day that has become your norm but at one time would have been considered innovative?

_____

_____

_____

_____

_____

_____

When you shut your mind down before it can even get started, you shackle your mind to a narrow existence. Allowing ourselves time to be bored is the best way to ignite our minds and imaginations. We are overstimulated from the moment we wake up to the second we lie down. Most of our stimulation is the byproduct of us living within the confines of someone else's imagination. You will never discover the power of your own ideas if you're constantly trapped living in someone else's.

You will never discover the power of your own ideas if you're constantly trapped living in someone else's.

Set aside ten minutes to free your mind in the direction of divine creativity. Start challenging yourself to redirect your creativity toward the direction of infinite possibilities. Jot down what comes up for you.

_____

_____

_____

_____

_____

What is one of the craziest problems in your world right now? Now write down positive solutions to the problem. Make sure the solution attaches in some way to your present reality.

_____

_____

_____

_____

_____

You don't know how God is going to solve your problems, but what if you started seeing everything in your life as a bridge to a miracle? How differently would you treat your circumstances? What peace would be immediately available to you? As you go through your week, take the time to start wildly imagining some possibilities.

INNOVATION MINDSET

Don't discredit the power of your curiosity to pave the way for innovation. You have an opportunity to innovate in your interpersonal relationships, financial and time management, and wellness goals.

Innovation is a muscle you can exercise each day if you're willing to think outside of defeat. Your mind is the most powerful weapon you possess. When nurtured properly it can empower you to unlock limitless potential. But with all its power, it's still relatively fragile, and with one experience or thought you can find yourself stagnant and distrusting of yourself.

When you transition to living with an innovation mindset, the impossible no longer feels too out of reach. The problems you see are opportunities for you to stretch your mind and establish new pathways for efficiency and success.

Think of an area of your life where you feel stuck right now. Let your mind run wild with possibilities of what it would take to change your reality. Journal your discoveries here.

_____

_____

_____

_____

_____

You'll know your innovation has the potential to be fruit-ful when it is rooted in gratitude for the present and a passion to thwart future problems before they even arise. When you innovate from a place of peace, your power maintains a healthy flow.

CHAPTER 14

CHANGING CONNECTIONS

**YOU DID NOT CHOOSE ME, BUT I CHOSE YOU
AND APPOINTED YOU THAT YOU SHOULD GO
AND BEAR FRUIT, AND THAT YOUR FRUIT
SHOULD REMAIN, THAT WHATEVER YOU ASK
THE FATHER IN MY NAME HE MAY GIVE YOU.**

JOHN 15:16

Our world is designed to reduce us to fit into particular categories. When people are trying to get to know you, most of them are trying to determine what type of person you are. Once they've done that, they build walls around you and expect you to stay in the category they understand.

One of the greatest gifts I've given myself is the freedom to be the complex creature God has created. I'm funny and serious. I am brave and afraid. I am powerful and insecure. I am strong and vulnerable. I am who I was, who I am, and who I am becoming all at the same time.

In what ways are you a complex, polarized figure?

I am _____ and _____.

I am _____ and _____.

I am _____ and _____.

When you refuse to live within the box people have relegated you to, you force relationships to be as fluid as the power you flow in. If a person is going to be connected with you, they're going to have to be able to move and flow as you do.

When you begin to put your power out there, you will be sounding an alarm to your friends, family, and community that you're flowing differently than you were before. When your innovation becomes more than a silly passing idea and turns into a powerful plan in motion, you will be able to see clearly who can flow with you and who can't go with you but has enough wisdom not to hold you back.

How do the people who flow with you support, expand, and restore you in the ways you need most?

_____

_____

_____

_____

_____

_____

There is going to come a time when your idea must be shared with someone. You need valuable input and various perspectives to help you understand what part of your concept is viable and what's underdeveloped. We all have blind spots, and valuable input offers us a more thorough view of how to position what's in our hearts to have maximum impact in the world.

When we choose to innovate in the ways of love, we're daring to ask the person we're committed to how to best show up for them in a way that matters the most to them.

How have you learned to show up for the people in your life?

_____

_____

_____

_____

_____

Make a list of your tasks and responsibilities. What do you desire to accomplish, and what do you legitimately have the capacity to accomplish? Do you really have to fulfill these obligations, or are you doing them because they're what you're supposed to do?

_____

_____

_____

_____

_____

_____

Take a moment to check your inner fuel tank. How far do you think you can go before running out of patience, energy, and hope today?

_____

_____

_____

_____

_____

Checking your inner fuel tank is a practice that sets the tone for your day, and the sooner you can get ahead of it, the better. If you can look at your life a couple of days or even a week in advance, you can better pace yourself. Once you assess what's realistic for you to accomplish, you can readjust expectations of those affected, and that's when the innovation begins.

WELCOMING INNOVATION

Real power can only exist when we flow in who God has called us to be.

How can you welcome innovation into the dynamics of how you relate with others?

_____

_____

_____

_____

_____

_____

_____

Real power can only exist when we flow in who God has called us to be.

There will be moments when there's no room for innovation, and all you can do is pray for the grace to survive the days ahead. In those moments I want to challenge you to get innovative with your prayers. Before turning to friends or family to help you, ask God, with specificity, to send His Spirit to guide you in the places you fear depletion.

My prayer life has increased in moments when my capacity does not measure up to the responsibilities at hand. Those are the moments I get to pray and ask the Holy Spirit to fill my cup and order my steps.

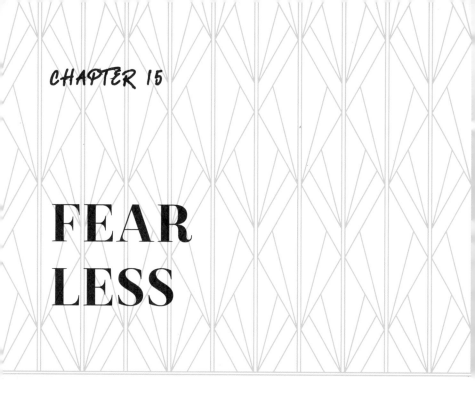

CHAPTER 15

FEAR
LESS

YOU ARE A CHOSEN GENERATION, A ROYAL PRIESTHOOD, A HOLY NATION, HIS OWN SPECIAL PEOPLE, THAT YOU MAY PROCLAIM THE PRAISES OF HIM WHO CALLED YOU OUT OF DARKNESS INTO HIS MARVELOUS LIGHT.

1 PETER 2:9

Being powerful is recognizing that your life is meant to fill the world with love and goodness no matter how much pain and bitterness you have experienced. Your life matters to God's master strategy of reconciling His creation back to Him.

The foundation of my faith is connected to my profound belief that following the life of Jesus is the only way to experience the fullness of God's plan for the earth and for me. When we model our lives after Jesus', as children of God, we no longer represent just ourselves, but we represent God too.

Many of us begin to suspect there is more to life than the moment we're drowning in. The pursuit of salvation has many impostors. Some look for it through achievement. Others search for it in substances. Some hunt for it in alcohol. And let's not forget about the ones who try to find it in love.

When you're feeling overwhelmed, where do you tend to turn for "salvation"?

_____

_____

_____

_____

_____

_____

_____

We find different saviors along the way, but none of them leave us satisfied until we discover a true relationship with Jesus. A relationship with Jesus is a fully integrated faith that begins with a curiosity, a "trial" period, and then finally a real commitment.

I'm not here to judge where you are on the journey, but I do want you to understand that the commitment stage of faith is not nearly as intimidating as choosing a spouse. With a partner, you may wonder how they'll think or feel if your most shameful secret is revealed. Jesus already knows you're raggedy. Jesus isn't expecting perfection. Jesus could not care less about your dirty little secrets. For some crazy reason, Jesus calls our scars beautiful and longs to see our slates wiped clean.

Ask God to reveal to you how radically He loves you. Journal here what He speaks to your heart.

_____

_____

_____

_____

_____

_____

How would it change your life to embrace the truth that God is not surprised by your success and is compassionate when you're at your worst?

_____

_____

_____

_____

_____

_____

We're almost at the end of this journey together, and I want nothing more than to set you up to make the type of power moves that free you from the pursuit of perfectionism. Life is a messy job. You get to decide whether you allow that mess to help you or bury you.

BECOMING A HEAVYWEIGHT

Each of us has come into this world with a weight to bear. Some of us may only have one burden, while others may have such a heavy load that it's bearing down on their shoulders. We all have moments when we become so distracted by what we're carrying that we miss out on the opportunity to make what we're carrying work for us.

What weights are you carrying?

_____

_____

_____

_____

How would it make a difference if you spent less time trying to get rid of the weight you're carrying and more time trying to figure out why God chose you to carry the weight in the first place?

_____

_____

_____

_____

You have to have a mindset that failure is not a blemish on your résumé but rather a brick on the road to your destiny. You are going to fail. You're going to be brilliant at some things and terrible at others. You're going to start off terrible in something and become a master the more you practice.

It's time to see past the devastation of failure and begin to see it as a necessary tool God uses to construct

Failure is not a blemish on your résumé but rather a brick on the road to your destiny.

who He knows you can become. What feels like a risk to you may be the only way you truly get to experience what God has placed inside you.

What failures have you experienced that left a mark on your confidence?

_____

_____

_____

STRADDLE THE LINE

While God is still revealing to you His plans and strategy for your future, you must trust and believe the clues are hidden in your present. Your relationship with disappointment and failure is critical in assuming a posture of power while you're waiting on God's plan to unfold.

Instead of seeing disappointment and failure as a delay or denial, where can you see them as divinely assigned to develop you for the future God has for you?

_____

_____

_____

What might God want to reveal to you about His character or yours today?

_____

_____

_____

_____

_____

I hold fast to the truth that we are to be in the world but not of it. Straddling that fence means there will be moments when we learn through mistakes and failure that we were leaning too far in one direction. Hindsight is a teacher that helps you to see clearly how to show up in power for your future.

The only win in life is living in a way that reflects God's image on earth. Don't allow your win to be determined by how well you performed. Instead lean into a mindset of victory anchored in how many lessons you've learned. When you are anxious for nothing, you can be present in the moment and open to the impossible.

CHAPTER 16

KNOW YOUR HARM

HE GIVES POWER TO THE WEAK, AND TO THOSE WHO HAVE NO MIGHT HE INCREASES STRENGTH.

ISAIAH 40:29

Like a well-meaning doctor, regardless of our intent, sometimes we may inflict harm on another individual. When we seek to move with power, we can only do so when we discern the power we've been granted can transform from a tool into a weapon and wound an undeserving soul.

Power without accountability will always turn into abuse. I believe this is why Jesus was intentional about taking time away from His close circle to have solitude with God. It wasn't just about the necessary refreshing and restoration that come from connecting with God.

How could prayer provide an opportunity for God to fine-tune your spirit when your actions are negatively impacting your ultimate goal or the people in your life?

_____

_____

_____

_____

Since most people find it hard to express disappointment, they internalize or suppress the way others' words and actions negatively affect them.

How safe do you think the people in your life feel about sharing the ways they experience disappointment in your behavior toward them?

_____

_____

_____

_____

Harnessing the power to be seen by others with all your beauty and flaws is one thing, but creating space for another imperfect person to share where you can be made whole is a skill that must be developed.

NO PERFECT TEACHERS

It takes multiple teachers for a student to become a master. Likewise, it takes multiple teachers for a person to become a force. Some teachers that God has assigned to your life are going to be imperfect.

Think of a time when someone who didn't have their life together gave you feedback. How did it strike you? How did you react?

_____

_____

_____

_____

_____

_____

What are some ways you could perform a quality-assurance check by opening lines of communication using direct questions to the people you're serving, leading, and connecting with? For example, instead of asking, "Do you think I'm a good friend?" you could ask, "Do you feel that I'm loyal to you and supportive of your work?"

_____

_____

_____

_____

Active accountability creates a culture where you can receive feedback about how you can improve. When a person knows you can handle the truth without punishing them, they feel safe enough to be authentic and corrected when needed.

Think of a word or phrase you could give to the people you're in relationship with to use when you're engaging in a harmful behavior you want to overthrow.

_____

_____

_____

If you feel uncomfortable about being this vulnerable, ask yourself this: *Would I rather hear about how my stress, insecurities, pride, or frustrations are negatively impacting the people in my life or feel it in the way they slowly drift away?*

There will be moments when you will feel ashamed of the way you've acted or communicated. What would it look like to survive the awkward vulnerability and come to see how the roots of your relationship have become deeper and richer?

POWER FORWARD

It takes just as much power to be held accountable for the way you cause harm as it does to move forward after you've been made aware of the ways you're still growing. This is where stillness, intentional introspection, and an intimate prayer life become your weapons and your healers. They are your weapons because they protect you from falling into an abyss of self-defeat, and they are your healers because they undergird a message that you will have to learn over and over: you can be powerful without being perfect.

Think of a time you hurt or offended someone. What were your thoughts, emotions, and actions? Consider how the way you harmed them was connected to unaddressed stress, fear, or anxiety. Journal about it here.

_____

_____

_____

_____

_____

_____

Another person's feedback tells you what you did, but introspection helps you understand how you were feeling and what you were thinking when you did it. I believe introspection is a powerful tool when accompanied with our prayers because it allows us to pour out our hearts to God.

Take some time to ask God to help you heal and express the thoughts that allowed the offense to occur in the first place. What is He revealing to you?

_____

_____

_____

_____

_____

_____

What would happen if you allowed your weakness to be what isolates you from connection? Conversely, what would happen if you saw your weakness as a runway to closer relationships?

_____

_____

_____

_____

_____

In 2 Corinthians 12, the apostle Paul was sharing with a church in Corinth what Jesus said to him when he admitted to struggling with the fact that he was undeniably anointed and called. Yet on the other hand Paul was so well acquainted with his weakness that he called it a "thorn in the flesh" (v. 7).

This is how Paul said Jesus responded to his dilemma: "He said to me, 'My grace is sufficient for you, for My strength is made perfect in weakness'" (v. 9). Paul's response to the knowledge of Jesus' strength being made perfect in him is revealed in the second part of the verse when Paul shared, "Therefore most gladly I will rather boast in my infirmities, that the power of Christ may rest upon me."

You can withstand the process of development that allows the power of Christ to rest upon you.

Don't allow the fact that you messed up to keep you down. If you're going to make a mistake, let those moments highlight just how far you are from being like God and how gracious God has been in extending you grace to make up the difference.

When is the last time you offered someone an apology for your behavior? Explore whether the behavior is a recurring pattern that has shown up in your life before.

_____

_____

_____

_____

_____

_____

_____

_____

If you're alive, the power of Christ can rest on you, imperfect as you may be, and make up the difference for the places where you fall short.

CHAPTER 17

SPREAD IT AROUND

THE LORD SAID TO SAMUEL, "DO NOT LOOK
AT HIS APPEARANCE OR AT HIS PHYSICAL
STATURE, BECAUSE I HAVE REFUSED HIM. FOR
THE LORD DOES NOT SEE AS MAN SEES; FOR
MAN LOOKS AT THE OUTWARD APPEARANCE,
BUT THE LORD LOOKS AT THE HEART."

1 SAMUEL 16:7

When Jesus first encountered a random man fishing in a sea, he didn't lure him away with promises of riches or fame. He didn't convince him that love and a pain-free life awaited him. Jesus simply made the man curious about how following Him could awaken an identity the fisher-man didn't know he possessed.

How much different would the world be if each person who has been awakened to and enlightened about the power they have to divinely effect lasting impact on the world made it their mission to awaken and enlighten others?

Don't gatekeep the areas where your power has been restored, lest you become like those who've led so many to believe that power is only reserved for a select few. The real sign of someone who is confident is not how they walk in the room. It's how they change every room they walk in for the better.

Jesus understood the more power you possess, the more you have to give away.

What would it look like in your life to trust that power is not in limited supply, that you can truly trust your connection to the All-Powerful? How might that help you not to be a hoarder but to look for ways to fill the cups of those who are struggling?

_____

_____

_____

_____

_____

The real sign of someone who is confident is not how they walk in the room. It's how they change every room they walk in for the better.

JUMP-START

When a car battery dies, there are only two ways for another car to jump-start it. Another driver in proximity can see the struggling driver and ask if they can help by giving the car a jump. Or the person who needs a jump can call someone nearby who can come to help them.

In either scenario there's one common denominator: proximity. That should be part of the criteria we use to gauge our ability to impart power into someone else's life.

Who around you could benefit from the grace in your life?

_____

_____

_____

_____

_____

_____

You could be the spark someone needs to realize their unique offering. I hear testimonies of people who are wondering what sets them apart. They don't fully trust there's anything about them that's worthy of distinction.

What has God placed inside you that could be a jump start to a person who is searching? How can you acknowledge how special their offering is and how they have greater impact than they realize?

_____

_____

_____

_____

_____

Jesus shows us that power is not to be reserved but rather poured into as many open and empty vessels as one can reach.

How can you intentionally create opportunities for other people to grow and develop?

_____

_____

_____

_____

_____

When someone encounters you, they're having a radical encounter with your authenticity and vulnerability. You should suspect you're carrying light with you wherever you go. Don't be surprised when people begin to say they feel better, calmer, and more hopeful once they've been in your presence.

GIVE WITHIN REASON

Sometimes we are so busy trying to make sure we pour into every person we meet that we don't take the time to observe if we're pouring into someone who is positioned so close to us that they're easy to overlook.

What are some traits of a person who can maximize the resource of you in their life?

_____

_____

_____

_____

_____

_____

Is there someone in your life who has demonstrated the ability to appreciate wisdom from other sources in the past? How did they do that?

_____

_____

_____

_____

If you're only investing in a person with the unspoken requirement that they will yield immediate transformation, it's actually manipulation. I will never understand why God gave His only begotten Son so that "whoever" believes in Him could have everlasting life (John 3:16). If I gave my only child for your salvation, you would not have an option on whether you believed. God demonstrates what it means to be a true giver. He gave His Son so that whosoever could have an *option*, not an *obligation*.

How does this truth speak to the heart posture in which God gave? What perspective should we imitate when giving?

_____

_____

_____

What can you afford to give of yourself whether someone appreciates it or not? That's the beginning of setting the boundaries for how you engage with others.

_____

_____

_____

_____

_____

_____

_____

THROW THE SEED

When we dismantle the paradigm that there's only room for one person of power, we can start to be active participants in creating space for the next wave of people to come. When God has granted you the ability to be powerful on earth, it is not diminished by another person stepping into their power. You must become an advocate with a mindset that says we need as many people to win as possible so we can shine with brilliance into dark places.

Can you think of a person who is just starting out with whom you can lavishly share your hard-earned lessons? How can you do that?

_____

_____

_____

_____

_____

_____

_____

_____

_____

_____

We cannot get a harvest where we have not planted seed. You want to see young people explore their passions and creativity? That's a great desire, but do you have any seed in the ground to cultivate that desire?

Make a list of the changes you want to see in your family, industry, friendships, or church. What seed do you have connected to those needs? Where could you throw more seed?

_____

_____

_____

_____

_____

_____

_____

_____

_____

If your outward presentation doesn't match your heart to see radical change in your relationships, profession, or community, then those around you will never have access to the inspiration that can make them better.

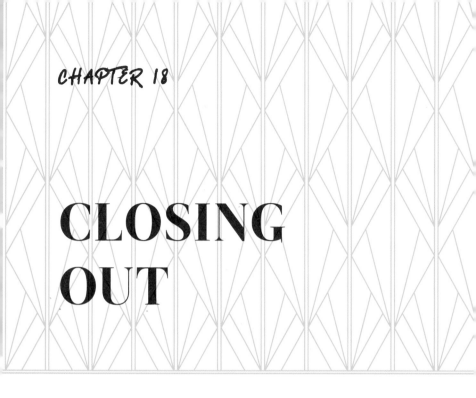

CHAPTER 18

CLOSING OUT

I HAVE FOUGHT THE GOOD FIGHT, I HAVE FINISHED THE RACE, I HAVE KEPT THE FAITH. FINALLY, THERE IS LAID UP FOR ME THE CROWN OF RIGHTEOUSNESS, WHICH THE LORD, THE RIGHTEOUS JUDGE, WILL GIVE TO ME ON THAT DAY, AND NOT TO ME ONLY BUT ALSO TO ALL WHO HAVE LOVED HIS APPEARING.

2 TIMOTHY 4:7–8

Staying power is not about staying on "top," wherever that may be. It's not about outachieving yourself or those around you. Those definitions of *staying power* eventually leave us lonely and deflated.

Collins Dictionary defines *staying power* as when "you have the strength or determination to keep going until you reach the end of what you are doing."[1] *Merriam-Webster* says staying power is the "capacity for continuing (as in existence, influence, or popularity) without weakening."[2] Each of these definitions leaves room for expiration. *Webster's* definition depends on never weakening, but it's humanly impossible to keep going physically without becoming weak. *Collins's* definition is intentional about adding that there must be an end to what you're doing.

I believe staying power is having the capacity to exercise strength or determination in trusting God without weakening. Power, in the ways I've unpacked for you, is not about you at all; it's about living your life as an ode to the Most High.

How can any of us truly stay powerful in the way that matters the most?

_____

_____

_____

We're the only thing God has created that runs the risk of living without the original power God intended us to possess. The sun, ocean, moon, and stars still take their place each morning and evening. Some days their brightness is more luminous than others. In some seasons they're hardly detectable at all, but never do they cease to have power. I want you to know that staying power for you will look different from season to season.

If you're fortunate enough to experience the privilege of age, staying power is not about how much youth you can keep clenched in your grasp. Staying power is about having faith that believes that no matter how old or irrelevant you may feel, you are not out of God's sight and can still be used for His plan.

Picture what it would look like for you to live authentically and actively seek God's heart and perspective on your truth. What would staying power look like in your life?

_____

_____

_____

_____

If you're going to finish strong at anything, you must stay connected to the ultimate Finisher. I don't know about you, but I don't want to finish as a hero in everyone else's eyes but be a failure at maximizing who God knew I could be.

It's especially hard for those of us who must analyze metrics to determine effectiveness. If your gauge for how effective or powerful you are is calculated with an algorithm, key performance indicators, reports, or feedback, you can easily fall into the trap of using someone else's

If you're going to
finish strong at
anything, you must
stay connected to the
ultimate Finisher.

criteria to determine your effectiveness. In some careers this cannot be avoided, but the metrics of your work, no matter how impressive or dismal, cannot determine the power of your being.

What are the metrics you tend to measure your success by?

_____

_____

_____

Where have you allowed the metrics of other people's opinions to determine whether you're powerful?

_____

_____

_____

How has feedback without God as your filter damaged your soul and thwarted your destiny?

_____

_____

_____

Spend a few minutes talking with God about the metrics He considers necessary. Ask Him to help you see where He is challenging you to remember that who you are is more important than what you can offer.

It's not always easy to see when you're allowing other people's metrics to determine how you feel about yourself, but my anxiety gives me a clue. When I feel anxious, that's when I know I'm moving away from authenticity and toward relentless productivity.

If there were no report to review, and the mouths that surround you were muted, how would you know in your soul that you finished strong? When life inevitably turns the page from one role to the next, how will you know you've walked away from that stage with power or lost your power in the transition?

Anytime you finish with a lesson that helps you see yourself more clearly and trust God more completely, you finish strong.

There is one final indicator of staying power: people who finish strong trust that doing it God's way, no matter how unique it is, is the only path to ultimate freedom. Find your confidence to be authentic. Trust that you can effect change. Don't you dare get stuck and stagnant, and do all that you can to ask for help when you've gone astray. Keep your heart open to the impossible and trust that you have the endurance to withstand the inevitable fears that come when you move in power.

Hope to see you in the flow.

NOTES

1. *Collins*, s. v. "staying power," accessed March 26, 2024, https://www.collinsdictionary.com/dictionary/english/staying-power.
2. *Merriam-Webster*, s. v. "staying power," accessed March 26, 2024, https://www.merriam-webster.com/dictionary/staying%20power.

ABOUT THE AUTHOR

Sarah Jakes Roberts is redefining what it means to be a modern woman of faith. Her messages spread throughout the world defying cultural, religious, gender, and socio-economic boundaries. Whether through her bestselling books or viral messages, it only takes a few minutes of connecting with her to understand why she has become an instant favorite. Sarah has a unique way of reaching people who are seeking to make peace with their past, maximize their present, and deepen their relationship with God.

Alongside her husband, Touré Roberts, she copastors at The Potter's House Church at ONE and also serves in leadership at The Potter's House Dallas. With her down-to-earth personality, contemporary style, and revelatory messages, there's no question about why she is an emerging thought leader for this generation.

BREAK UP WITH YOUR FEARS AND REVOLUTIONIZE YOUR LIFE.

WOMAN EVOLVE

NO WOMAN LEFT BEHIND GUIDED JOURNAL

VISIT WOMANEVOLVEBOOK.COM TO LEARN HOW.

ALSO AVAILABLE BY SARAH JAKES ROBERTS

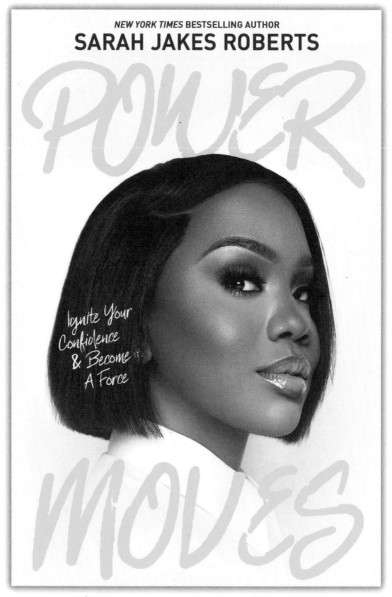